Emot Intelligence

The Guide You Need to Have a Better Life. Improve Your Social Skills and Emotional Agility, Overcome Anxiety, Stress and Depression, and Raise Your EQ

Richard Hawkins

The information in the following pages is broadly considered to be a truthful and accurate account of facts and as such any inattention, use or misuse of the information in question by the reader will render any resulting actions solely under their purview. There are no scenarios in which the publisher or the original author of this work can be, in any fashion, deemed liable for any hardship or damages that may befall them after undertaking information described herein. The author does not take any responsibility for inaccuracies, omissions, or errors which may be found therein.

Additionally, the information in the following pages is intended only for informational purposes and should thus be thought of as universal. As befitting its nature, it is presented without assurance regarding its prolonged validity or interim quality. The author of this work is not responsible for any loss, damage, or inconvenience caused as a result of reliance on information as published on, or linked to, this book.

The author of this book has taken careful measures to share vital information about the subject. May its readers acquire the right knowledge, wisdom, inspiration, and succeed.

Table of Contents

Introduction

Congratulations on downloading this book and thank you for doing so. The following chapters will teach you how to achieve mastery over your social life, as well as how you can turn yourself into a powerful social magnet:

- Chapter 1 gives the guidelines on putting all the techniques together and achieving mastery.

- Chapter 2 teaches the Master's Techniques that will allow you to ignite your social life and take it to the highest level.

- Chapter 3 talks about the best practices of socializing in order to increase your chances of success.

- Chapter 4 lays down the common pitfalls that you should avoid.

May this book be your guiding light to a happy and meaningful social life.

There are plenty of books on this subject on the market, so thanks again for choosing this one! Every effort was made to ensure it is full of as much useful information as possible. Please enjoy!

Chapter 1: Master Guidelines

Putting It All Together

Now that you have reached the last part of the series on social improvement, it is time for you to learn the master's techniques that will completely turn you into a powerful social magnet. This is about taking all the techniques that you already know, putting them together, and even taking them to the next level.

By now, you should already have a good grasp of the basic and advanced techniques. This book will show you how to apply them all in your day-to-day life and help you attract more people to expand your social circle. When you put together all the techniques, then it means that you already have, at least, a good grasp of them and are able to apply them in your life. It is worth noting that you should not rush the development process. Feel free to go back to the previous books and reviews the different techniques and strategies. It should also be noted that you do not need to attain a high level of mastery over the techniques before you can use this book. In fact, this book is about helping you gain mastery over the techniques and strategies that we have discussed in the previous books in the series.

Putting all the techniques together simply means that you should make use of applicable techniques all at once when possible. You do not literally apply all the techniques in one moment, but only what is possible under certain circumstances.

A common mistake is to attempt to learn all of the techniques at once. Again, it is not good to rush the development process. Learning the techniques takes time and practice. If you rush the process, then there is a good chance that you will only fail as a result. You must give yourself enough time to adjust and get used to the techniques. Soon enough, the techniques will become a natural part of you. For starters, it is recommended that you learn the techniques one by one. Once you get used to the practice, then you can add another technique, and then another.

The key is not to be hard on yourself. Just learn as much as you can and do so at a comfortable pace. Take note, however, that this book teaches how you can effectively combine all the basic techniques, so you might want to review the basics before you read this book further, especially if you do not have a good grasp of the basic and advanced techniques yet. You do not need to immediately attain mastery, as this book is the guide that will teach you how to gradually achieve mastery over the techniques.

The techniques are not separate from one another. This is something that you haven't yet realized. The techniques, although they may appear different, actually compose a whole system of effective social interaction and connection.

The key to achieving mastery is to focus on the individual components of the system. Hence, you have to work on individual techniques. After which, you need to learn to combine and apply them altogether. This is the way to achieve mastery, and the only step to do this is by acquiring the right knowledge and expanding upon what you know through continuous practice.

Taking It a Step Further

As this is the master's guide to social improvement, this is the time to take the techniques that you already know beyond the border. This is an important step as it is what distinguishes a real expert from someone who merely knows the techniques. If you want to take your social skills to a level that will actually draw people towards you, then this is the book that you need.

Taking the techniques a step further is not really that complicated. It is a matter of working on your weaknesses and learning to combine the different techniques and applying them naturally in your day-to-day dealings and interactions. As for your strengths, you should try to develop them further, if possible. This is the first step on the path to perfection. If you think that you already know the techniques as discussed in the previous books, then this master's manual will give you a new direction for continuous improvement.

Just like with the other books in the series, don't be too hard on yourself when you're trying to apply the techniques in this book. It is worth remembering that improving one's social life should be fun and give you a nice experience. Of course, you may experience some disappointments from time to time, especially when you meet difficult and negative people, but the overall experience should be positive in nature. After all, as discussed in the previous book, improving your social life is a path of self-discovery and realization. This is a process that is full of self-discovery and new things you can learn about.

Taking the techniques a step further also means bringing yourself to a new level and experience. This also entails new challenges and lessons that you can learn along the way. Always keep an open mind and learn as much as you can. Again, don't be too hard on yourself and never give up even if you are met with failures and disappointments. As you can see, it is not just the techniques that you will take a step further but yourself. Again, this is all about you and a way to make yourself grow as a person. So, if you are ready for another new adventure to self-discovery and realization, as well as an effective way to expand your social circle, then this book is your number one guide.

Becoming a Social Magnet

By the time that you finish this book together with all the other books in the series, then you will already have the right foundation and understanding of becoming a social magnet. It is all just matter of putting your knowledge into actual practice.

Being a social magnet, you can easily attract people and create strong connections with them. Take note that this should not be used as a way to manipulate people but to create good and lasting relationships. As you may already know, improving your social life is not about pleasing others or controlling them, but it is about becoming a better person and forming good relationships with people so that you can live a happier and more meaningful life.

Becoming a social magnet is not a complicated process. It is mostly about knowing the techniques and applying them in your life. Now, the first part of this process is usually not a problem. If you read this book and the other books in the series, then you will already be equipped with the right knowledge; however, the real challenge is putting your newfound knowledge into continuous practice. In this case, you need to change and change is not always easy as it is quite difficult to break bad habits, much less to replace them with good and positive habits. However, the good news is that this is doable and that you are the only person who can do this.

You will notice that the master's techniques in this book mirror the techniques in the other books in the series. This is because this book teaches how you can attain mastery of all the techniques (basic and advanced techniques). Perhaps there is nothing new that you will learn except that how you can combine and apply the techniques more effectively, and this is an important step to take in achieving perfection.

Think about how your life would be once you turn yourself into a real social magnet. Imagine having positive relationships with different people and having a respectable social image. See yourself enjoying life with others and living a life that is full of harmony, kindness, peace, and especially love. After all, one cannot attain peace and kindness when he is alone; for one to say that they know what love is, then it has to be shared with another, for love cannot exist when you are alone.

However, as a social magnet, you will also draw difficult people towards you from time to time. This is why you need to learn to effectively filter the people in your circle. Do not forget that in building a social circle, quality is more important than quantity. It is better to have two nice and good people in your circle than 20 arrogant 'friends' who only think about themselves. But, if you apply the techniques properly, then you will most likely draw the right kind of people to join your circle. As the saying goes, "Like attracts like."

Becoming a social magnet is well within your reach; however, it does not happen overnight. Just like anything that is worth learning or having, you need to dedicate time and effort before you can master the techniques. Without further ado, let us discuss the master's techniques that can turn you into a real social magnet.

Chapter 2: Master's Techniques

The First Encounter

This is about making a good and lasting impression. Every new relationship starts with a first meeting or encounter. By now, you are expected to be familiar with the basic and advanced techniques. So, what do you do on your first meeting? Take note that this is where you make your first impression. At the same time, the other person will also have to make his or her impression on you. These days, people no longer pay attention to the importance of making a good impression. Although it is true that you do not have to please people, it is still important to project the right social image, especially if you do not know so much about each other. This is also a good way to avoid any misunderstanding between the two parties.

On the first encounter, it is a good practice to give a friendly greeting, smile, and to shake the other person's hand. Do not wait for him or her to hold out their hand. Instead, extend your hand and be the one to initiate the action. This kind gesture is very simple and easy to do yet there are still those who fail to observe it. A common obstacle is shyness. As we have already discussed in the previous book in the series, you should not be shy if you want to improve your social life. However, just a reminder, there is a difference between being shy and being arrogant. You must learn to be confident and humble at the same time.

Friendliness and being cheerful can make you project a quality of being approachable. Hence, cultivate a friendly attitude, especially on your first meeting. Also, avoid saying anything that is negative. When the person you talked thinks about their encounter with you, he or she should not be reminded of anything that has a negative nature. So, keep all things positive and light. This will also make the other person feel good and comfortable when talking with you. Here is a secret: The quality of your conversation usually describes the quality of the experience itself. Therefore, by making the conversation light and positive, the experience will also have a positive vibe. As you can see, this reveals the key to making a good and lasting impression.

The problem with messing up the first encounter is that the other person might filter you out immediately to the point that he or she would no longer see the real you. Do not forget that social life is not just about you but also involves other people. Now, as to how other people think or feel, that is something that is outside of your control. You cannot force people to add you to their social circle. However, by improving yourself and becoming a better person, people would want to add you to their circle. This is why it is important to improve one's self.

But, what if you mess up the first encounter? Well, the only option you have would be to do better next time so that the other person would consider joining you again. However, as already mentioned, the problem with messing up the first encounter is that you might not have another chance to prove yourself. Therefore, as much as possible, try to make a good and lasting first impression.

It is clear that by being well-manned, you can make a good first impression, but how do you make a lasting first impression? Here is something that you should understand: All good first impressions can be lasting first impressions. It is all a matter of how you make yourself more relevant in the mind of the person. Now, there is no hard and fast rule on this matter but more about the chemistry that you create. Although there is no guaranteed way to create a positive chemistry with everyone, it is worth noting that the techniques in this book, as well as in the other books in the series, can significantly help you create good and lasting first impressions as these techniques form the fundamentals of a good relationship.

Now, what if it is you who is not interested in the other person? Just because you are not interested in the other person does not mean that you no longer have to be nice to them. Also, if you truly realize the meaning of the teachings in these books in the series, you should know by now that you act kindly because you are kind and not for the sole purpose of expanding your social circle.

Indeed, improving one's social life is also about improving one's self.

Just as you can make mistakes and project a negative impression on the first meeting, you should also be considerate of other people. Do not quickly write off people out of your list just because of a bad first impression. Do not hesitate to give people another chance. Again, keep an open mind and be kind.

Active Listening

Active listening itself is a recurring topic throughout the books in the series. This is because it is a very important technique that you should learn. Without knowing how to listen properly, it would be difficult to create good and lasting relationships. Keep in mind that in a relationship, communication is vital; and in communication, listening is the most important skill. Since this is the master's guide, you should apply all the techniques of active listening at once, when possible. For example, make eye contact as you ask questions in a conversation. Another example is to repeat what the other person has just told you, and then follow it up with a question that will help the other person to further explain themselves.

Listening should also be done with sincerity. If you find it hard to listen since you are not interested in the topic of the conversation, at least try to listen out of your interest in or respect for the person who is talking to you.

The next time that you talk with someone consciously and deliberately make an effort to listen more and talk less. You will find that by listening more to what others have to say, you can improve the quality of the conversation. Of course, this does not mean that you cannot share your own thoughts and ideas. Rather, this only means that you should also give other people a chance to express themselves. Unfortunately, there are people out there who only want to be heard and do not want to hear others. Keep in mind that true and effective communication is a two-way process. The parties need to take turns between talking and listening. It is advised that you should spend more time with listening. If you listen more, then you can talk more effectively.

Do not just listen to the words, but also pay attention to how a person talks, their gestures, eye movements, expressions, and others. The truth is that the whole body communicates, or at least it conveys a message. After all, words are just symbols that signify how a person thinks or feels. Pay attention to the little things, and you will be able to better understand the other person. Indeed, listening is the key to an effective communication.

It would be difficult to listen if the other person does not talk or is not open enough. This is why you also have to encourage them to talk by asking more questions. The key is to help the other person to express themselves. The more the other person expresses themselves and is open to you and the more that you listen, the better the connection will be.

A common mistake is to think that people who open up to you are only looking for answers or solutions to their problems. Of course, it would be helpful if you can always offer a solution, but this is not always the case. The truth is that many of these people just want someone who would listen to them — someone they feel that they could open up to and not judge them. They want someone who would listen to them and at least try to understand them. Fortunately, this is something that you can do. Indeed, effective listening is the key to building a good and meaningful relationship.

Effective Mirroring

As we have discussed in the previous book in the series, mirroring techniques are where you imitate the body language of the person whom you are talking with. This is a subtle yet effective way to make a connection. It also allows you to empathize with the person more effectively. As a master's technique, mirroring should be combined with asking the right questions and the art of listening. You should be able to apply mirroring naturally without calling any attention to how you mirror the gestures or actions of the other person. Also, do not forget that you should never allow the other person to have any idea that you are mirroring him or that you are using any social techniques. Everything should be performed naturally without attracting undue attention. People would not like it if they know that you are applying techniques on them as if you were manipulating them, so be discrete when you use the techniques.

It should be noted that proper timing is also essential. Mirroring should be applied in the middle of the conversation. You should use it a few minutes before you want to influence the other person and be more connected with them. Also, do not forget that mirroring is just one part of the process. After physically mirroring the other person, you should express a thought or idea that has the power to persuade. If you are able to persuade the other person, the next step is to break the 'mirror' by changing your gesture or hand positioning and see if the other person would follow you. This time it is the other person who would be mirroring you, but he or she should not be conscious of it. When you see this happen, then that is a clear sign that they are now more open to your suggestions.

Now, a common mistake is that there are people who effectively apply mirroring but fail to take advantage of it. You should realize that this technique actually has four parts: The first part is where you physically mirror the other person. The second part is where you present a dominating or persuading thought or idea. The third part is where you break the mirror and the other person becomes the one who is following you or mirroring you unconsciously, and the fourth and last part is where the other person is already open to suggestion and you continue to feed them with your own thoughts and ideas and also connect with them on a higher level.

Take note that once the other person ends up mirroring you, then you should grab that opportunity and feed them with your thoughts and opinions on the subject. It is the best opportunity to influence them and make them think and feel the way you want them to. However, just like the other techniques, it is noteworthy that you should not use this as a way to control people; rather, this technique is given to you so that you can use it to improve your relationship with people. Indeed, in applying the techniques in this book and all the other books in the series, your intention also counts. Keep in mind that one's intention also says a lot about one's sincerity.

There is one gesture that you should not mirror, and that is when a person crosses their arms and or legs. This act of crossing usually signifies a defensive position, which is counterproductive to your objective. As much as possible, you want the other person to be open to you. So, what do you do if the person seems to be too defensive and closed? Well, the best course of action is to keep asking questions. Needless to say, you also should not mirror those gestures that have a disrespectful and offensive nature, such as rolling the eyes, and others.

An advanced style of mirroring goes beyond copying gestures and physical actions. This kind of mirroring is where you also mirror how a person talks. Now, be careful about this technique as you cannot let the other person notice you doing it. And, no, you do not have to change your voice or do anything hilarious; however, you will have to talk just like the other person by seeing this from their perspective and using their own ideas. In a way, this is just about saying and affirming the other person's ideas. Although this may seem quite strange, it should be noted that many people out there just want to be with people who could affirm or support what they already know. This is how a person will see you less of a threat and more of a friend. He or she will think and feel that you're two birds of the same 'feather' and would like to 'flock' with you. A sense of empathy is needed to apply this technique, and you can do this by placing yourself in the shoes of the person with whom you are interacting with. Consider their perspective on the subject and try to find out more about their interests. This will allow you to tackle the subject more effectively.

The Art of Asking Questions

This is a very important master's technique that you should learn. The art of asking questions is the key to developing the conversation, and it is also related to the art of listening. Indeed, these techniques should be applied all at once for the best result. So, what is this art of asking questions? As you already know, you should not ask a question just for the sake of asking a question. Rather, you must ask the right questions. What are the right questions? They are the questions that help develop the conversation. In other words, they refer to the questions that encourage the other person to talk, be open, and share their thoughts, feelings, and ideas, with you.

Learning to ask the right questions require plenty of practice. An important thing to note is to use it to direct and develop the flow of conversation. It should also be performed naturally; otherwise, the other person might feel that you are interrogating them, and that would make them uncomfortable.

This is not hard to do. The secret lies in listening. If you listen to what the other person tells you, then it will be easy for you to ask the right questions. You simply have to follow their train of thoughts and flow of the conversation. Stop thinking about yourself and direct your interest towards the other person. The more that you listen, the more that you can ask the right questions; and the more that you ask the right questions, the more that the person will feel comfortable with you as he or she would feel comfortable opening up to you. These days, it is simply not that easy to find a person with whom you would feel comfortable talking about your thoughts and emotions without having to worry that he or she might judge you.

As you can see, you do not even have to be knowledgeable. In fact, there are times when you do not even have to know anything about the subject of the conversation; but by asking relevant questions, you can still engage in a meaningful conversation. Not to mention, there are many people out there who feel good and pleased when they talk about and share what they already know. Indeed, there are those who simply want to talk and be heard. When you use the art of questioning, be sure to apply it together with active listening.

If you yet to establish a level of closeness with a person, then you should be cautious of the questions that you ask. Do not make the other person feel that you are invading their personal space. The key is never to force a person to open up to you but simply to convince them that you are someone they can trust. Of course, the way to effectively do this is by applying the techniques.

Words of Power

You should be careful with how you use your words. Words have power. Unfortunately, many people do not know how to use words effectively and get stuck with shallow conversations or little talks. Take note that there is nothing wrong with engaging in little talks, but you should not be content with them. You must, whenever possible, develop the conversation. By developing the level of conversation, you can also improve your relationship with the person you're talking with.

The truth is that words do have power. However, the extent of this power will depend on how you make use of these words. Be clear and straightforward in all your conversations. Also, be careful with how you use your words. A good exercise that you can do is to list down statements or lines that you often use. Now, try to come up with a better version of that statement. This is how to be more effective in using words. By improving your choice of words, you can also increase the power of your speech. This can all lead to a better level of communication. In turn, better communication creates good relationships.

It is important for you to learn how to use words effectively as they are your primary tool in expressing your thoughts and ideas to people. Words also have the power to evoke emotions in people. Now, this is something that takes time and effort to learn. There are many ways to express yourself using words and the manner of conveying your thoughts also matter.

Words of power can put the other person at ease and make them feel comfortable talking with you. You do not have to come up with an intricate or complicated combination of words. In fact, it is suggested that you stick to simple yet direct statements, such as "Tell me more," or "Is there anything I can do to make you feel better?" Needless to say, you should use such statements sincerely. Without sincerity, the other person would not feel good at all about the conversation.

Instead, he or she will put up walls, and this would be counterproductive to your efforts.

You should make it a habit to pay attention to how other people talk, especially with respect to their choice of words. If you find someone who makes you feel comfortable and easily gains your trust, ask yourself what it is about that person that makes you feel so light inside and what about them made you more willing to open up. Pay attention to the words that these kinds of people use, as well as the manner that in which they communicate with you. There is so much that you can learn from people. Now, in case that you end up talking with a difficult person, you can still draw lessons from the experience. Ask yourself what it is about the person that makes them difficult to get along with. Does he or she use offensive language or expressions? Or is it simply their manner of talking? By doing this, you will know specific points that you want to avoid. Now, combining them all together, you will be able to know the qualities that you should reinforce and also those that you should exclude.

Expanding Your Social Circle

Improving your social life also involves expanding your social circle, and this means adding more people in your circle. Although you may already feel content and satisfied with your current set of friends, it does not mean that you can no longer develop and expand your circle. In fact, it is encouraged that you take steps to expand your circle and meet new interesting people. This, of course, is still a matter of personal preference. The reason why this is encouraged is that it is a helpful way to grow as a person and learn even more. Sometimes a person may think that his or her current circle is all that there is in a social life, without realizing that social living means so much more if only he or she had not limited themselves to this current circle. By expanding your circle, you get to meet other people and learn from them. Just as there is no end to self-development, there is also no end to improving one's social life.

Expanding your social life is just as simple as continuously applying the basic techniques: Be open, get to know more people, actively listen to a person when he talks, be kind and approachable, among many others. The key is not to stop but to always seek continuous improvement.

Of course, expanding one's social circle has its risks. You open the risk of meeting negative and difficult people. But, this is also the reason why you should apply effective filtering. The thing is that if you do not expand your circle simply because you want to avoid the aforesaid risk, then you are also preventing yourself from meeting nice and interesting people.

Master the Art of Filtering

The art of filtering is a way to take control of the people that you allow to join in your circle. Now, it is easy to say that you should filter and choose those that you welcome into your circle, but how do you actually go about doing it?

You should be careful with filtering your connections. After all, you do not want to offend anyone or give them a message that you do not like them or that you simply do not want them to be in your life. The best approach is to keep a distance from people who you want to filter out. Actually, you do not have to completely remove them from your social circle. Instead, you can manage your connections and simply keep a distance from those who might not fit your preference. This way you are not sending people away. Not to mention, people also change and there are those who, like yourself, can change for the better. It just really takes time for this to happen.

The best way to filter out undesirable people is simply by giving them less time and attention. If you spend less time with them, their effect on your life will weaken, and then finally it will be as if they do not exist in your circle. You should avoid spending time with them. If they invite you to a meeting, learn to say *no* in a polite and respectful manner. You do not have to be rude towards rude people. Otherwise, you will end up just like them. Stay close to good people and avoid those who do not help you grow as a person, but do your best to learn what you can from them.

Improving your social life is a continuous journey of learning and self-discovery. Do not place any limitation on your social life. Meet as many interesting and strange people as you can. Learn from every meeting, person, and experience. The more that you expand your social life, the more that you will know and understand yourself. This is the way to self-improvement, which is also the way to improving your social life.

How to Get Along with Difficult People

Getting along with difficult people is a real challenge when it comes to becoming more social. Although you can filter out people that you don't like, there will still be occasions when you cannot avoid interacting with difficult and negative people. Still, you should learn how to get along with them.

Other than the techniques in the previous books on how you can handle difficult people, an important thing to take note of is to have a better understanding of yourself. The more that you know yourself, the easier it will be for you to deal with difficult people. Keep in mind that just because you are dealing with a difficult person does not mean that you should also act in a negative manner. Rather, remind yourself who you are and just be yourself. Realize that you are in no way connected by others. Do not be attached to them, especially to negative people.

If a difficult person is making it hard for you to reign in your anger, learn to delay your reaction. As we have discussed in the previous book, by delaying your response time, you can gain more control of yourself and you will not be overcome by destructive emotions. Getting along with difficult people is mostly about not allowing yourself to be like them. When they move you to become angry or disappointed, know that you always have a choice whether you will allow yourself to feel and act negatively.

Do not expect or hope for difficult people to change easily. That is something outside of your control. Instead, just be who you are. Sometimes by simply being kind to them, even difficult people learn and change on their own. When you interact with such people, it is just a matter of whose personality will prevail. Be yourself and do not let other people change who you are.

Learn to Say No

This is considered a master technique since many people find it hard to simply say *no*. They think that by saying no, you are rejecting someone. This is not always the case. In fact, you have to understand that saying *no* can also be considered a virtue. Sometimes, it is even more important than saying *yes*, especially during times when you really have to turn down someone.

It is noteworthy that saying *no* is not really about turning down or rejecting anyone; rather, it is about being honest with yourself and other people. Saying *no* is also an effective way to set a limit so that you would not be abused by people.

It is better, to be honest, and say *no* than to say *yes* without actually meaning what you are saying. Again, sincerity is very important in building a good relationship, and this remains true even when you have to say *no*.

If you want to be polite, then you may want to give a reason for saying *no*, so that the other person will not feel offended. For example, you can say, *"No, because..."* However, it is also noteworthy that you do not have to give any reason. Yes, you read that right — you do not have to explain yourself to anyone. Hence, if you have to say *no*, then just say *no* and do not worry about it. But, of course, you should also be careful every time you use this word as it might offend a person. Before you turn someone down, consider the circumstances first.

Now, if after giving it consideration you feel like you must really say *no*, then learn to do so without hesitation.

Increasing Intimacy

The more intimate the relationship is, the stronger the connection becomes. You should understand that intimacy cannot exist without chemistry. Now, for there to be chemistry, there must be a mutual relationship between the two parties. Take note that a mutual relationship does not only refer to a relationship between two people; rather, there is mutual understanding between them. In a good relationship, there must be trust and confidence.

Once there is a good relationship, then it will be easier to improve the quality of the relationship. An effective way of becoming more intimate is by getting more personal. You can do this by connecting to the person on a deeper level. Depending on the circumstances, this is the time to talk and share each other's problems, secrets, dreams, fears, and others. The more personal and intimate the conversation is, the stronger the relationship becomes. It is noteworthy that once you reach this level, trust plays a very important role. Remember that once trust is broken, a good relationship can easily fall apart. So, be true and remain trustworthy at all times.

The more intimate a relationship is, the stronger it becomes. It is worth noting that this intimacy is not the same with the intimacy found in a man-woman relationship. Intimacy can exist even between friends, even of the same sex. This has nothing to do with a romantic kind of relationship. Rather, it is about increasing the trust and confidence shared by both parties in a good relationship.

Self-Discovery and Realization

The whole journey of social living is a process of self-discovery and realization. If you approach it the right way, it allows you to grow more as a person and improve yourself. As a master's technique, do not just focus on other people but also focus on yourself. Think about your present relationships and ask yourself: What are the things or qualities that you have that you can further improve or develop? The next step is to come up with positive actions that you need to do in order to work on said possible developments. Positive actions are important as they allow beneficial changes to take effect. Without taking positive actions, an actual change would be impossible.

When you develop your social life, you also have to improve yourself. This is the most important and integral part of the process. Indeed, these days, so many people have been controlled by the demands of modern life and society that they forget who they really are. Instead, they are misdirected by the media, the news, and others, that show

how you should live your life instead of how you want to live your life. Instead of being true to themselves and to others, many people learn to project false images and illusions of themselves. By doing so, they fail to truly live a meaningful life. They become a product of society instead of making society reflect who they are. This is why having the right approach to improving your social life is very important. Otherwise, you will live an empty existence at the expense of your own life and happiness. A good and enjoyable social life is one that will allow you to be who you are and live your life the way you want.

Be Yourself

Always be yourself. This is an important teaching. We have already discussed this in the previous book, and it is worth repeating again and again. You do not improve your social life by pleasing other people. The right way is to be yourself and attract and welcome the right people into your circle.

Always be true to yourself. It is also the only way to be true to other people. If your life to yourself, then you also lie to others by not showing them who you really are.

It should be made clear that being yourself does not mean that you can just act any way you want without any form of discipline or control. That is acting foolishly and not being yourself. When you are yourself, then that is where complete freedom is, where you freely express who you are. Of course, for this to become possible, you must first realize who you are. Again, other people can help you realize your self-identity. Remember the '*Parable of the White Room*' in the previous book? It signifies just how socializing can help you realize your true self. Also, realize that true freedom is not about doing whatever you want, but it is being yourself without fear and without having to please other people.

When you are yourself, you can express your thoughts and ideas effectively. Also, it is only when you are true to yourself that you can be really happy. This is why it is important to be yourself. But, of course, you cannot just be who you ever you are or act carelessly. An important rule you should keep in mind is that you must also improve yourself and develop your personality. This means that you should learn to be respectful, polite, and kind. Remember that other people also have rights that you should respect. Just as you can be yourself, you should also allow other people to be themselves. In fact, people will start to think it's good to have you in their company if you're the type of person that helps people be who they truly are.. Needless to say, this will persuade them into thinking that having a good relationship with you is beneficial. But, of course, this is only possible if they feel comfortable in your company; hence, you also have to improve yourself.

Thought Control and Discipline

This technique has more to do with yourself than other people. This is about having the discipline to control your thoughts. As mentioned in the previous book: "The happiness of your life depends upon the quality of your thoughts." This is not a unique saying. In fact, it was taken from a known Stoic named Marcus Aurelius, a Roman emperor. This teaching also applies if you want to improve your social life.

Now, how do you exactly control your thoughts? This is not some form of meditation where you need to still your mind. Rather, controlling your thoughts simply means that you should be the one to direct your thoughts and not the other way around. It also means that you should exercise the power to keep your thoughts positive. If you fill your mind with positive thoughts, then you can also act positively. The contrary is true for the opposite.

This is how your thoughts can influence you, as well as the people around you. Needless to say, this has a lot to do with the way that you experience life. In fact, your mood is strongly influenced by your thoughts. As an experiment, spend about 15 minutes doing nothing but thinking about the people whom you do not like. After the said time, assess yourself how you feel. Chances are that you would not feel good and that even your mood would be affected. Now, do the contrary and think about the people who make you happy. After which, reassess yourself and how you feel. This is a good exercise to test just how the quality of your thoughts can affect you as a person, including your state of mind.

This does not mean that you should no longer deal with problems and stress; however, it only means that you should control how you deal with negative things and emotions. You can do this by taking control of your thoughts. Now, do not expect to learn this technique quickly. In fact, this is one of the techniques in this book that is not that easy to learn. The good news is that it is doable provided that you devote enough time and practice. You should also have the discipline to practice this technique regularly. Indeed, it is not that easy to break a bad habit, especially when it concerns the mind. However, with repeated practice, there is no technique that you cannot master.

Law of Attraction

This law has become very popular, especially in the modern times. According to this 'universal' law, 'like attracts like.' Hence, if you are a good person, then you tend to attract good people. Conversely, if you are rude or offensive, then you also tend to attract negative people into your life. What this means is that by changing or controlling who you are, you can affect your reality.

If you come to think about it, there is really nothing strange or magical about this law. Rather, it draws its power and truth directly from human nature. When you are kind to a person, that person will most likely treat you kindly as well. This is a liberal rule that all religions preach. Remember the golden rule: "Do unto others as you would have them do unto you." Now, this may not always work 100% of the time, but you can expect for this to work most of the time and that is what matters — that it works and that you can make a positive difference.

Plenty of books can be written about the law of attraction. With respect to building a good social life, what you should remember is that by improving yourself, you can improve the things that are around you, and this includes the people in your circle. This is not a universal law, but more has to do with human nature and instinct. Good and kind people like those who are also kind and nice, and they avoid loud and offensive people. Hence, by improving yourself, you can attract the right people into your life.

The best effect of this law of attraction happens when two people apply it at the same time. If these two people meet, and they both have positive qualities, a strong bond and a positive relationship can be created. Of course, from time to time, you may still attract the wrong people, but that is part of the risk. Do not worry, you will also draw the right people and that is what is important. When you do find someone whom you can trust, it is advised that you take the effort to connect with him. Indeed, it is not that easy to find a friend whom you can completely trust. Also, the relationship should be mutual in the sense that both parties must benefit from the relationship. This does not refer to any monetary benefit but has more to do with being happy and content with your life.

Although there are skeptics out there who do not believe in the law of attraction, there are those who put their faith in this law. As far as this book is concerned, you do not really have to believe in the law of attraction as some form of magical force. Rather, just consider it as some form of cause and effect relationship. When you are nice, you tend to draw nice people; but when you are rude and offensive, kind people would stay away from you.

Chapter 3: Best Practices

Respect

Respect plays an important role in any relationship. Without respect, it would be difficult for a relationship to work. As a rule, you should always respect everyone — no exceptions. If you respect others, they will most likely also respect you in return. Now, if they do not respect you, you can still take comfort in the fact that at least you are not like them. When you connect and interact with people, you should always be respectful in your words and deeds. Without respect, it is impossible to build a good relationship.

Respect even your enemies, for even enemies, can show each other respect.

It is not good to be disrespectful as it forms a basic quality of being a human. When a person talks, then you should listen. When you talk, do not offend the other person. It is a fundamental element in any relationship. Hence, if you lack respect, then it will really be hard, if not impossible, to build a meaningful relationship.

You do not always have to agree with another person. However, when you express your disagreement, it is important that you do not forget to show respect. In fact, in everything that you do, make sure that you do not disrespect anyone. It is when you lose respect that relationships can become a problem. But, if you respect everyone, people will appreciate it and would want to have a good relationship with you. Unfortunately, in today's world, so many people are disrespectful and take it as if it were a sign of independence. Fortunately, when you are respectful enough, people appreciate it. Now, in case nobody notices your efforts, do not be discouraged. After all, it is enough to know that you are respectful. Again, you do not socialize to please other people. If someone in your circle is pleased, then consider it a bonus. It is enough that you know that you are respectful and that you can have a clear conscience.

Talk About the Other Person's Interest

An entire book can be written about this practice: Talk about the other person's interest. This is an essential tip if you want to win friends and influence people. By talking about the other person's interest, you get to 'entertain' them and they will feel good talking with you. You make them feel comfortable, pleased, and happy. This is not hard to do considering that most people are more likely to open up if you want to talk about their interests. In fact, people want to talk about their interests. It is just a matter of meeting someone who would allow them to talk and enjoy the conversation. The good news is that *someone* could be you.

When you want to follow this approach, the art of listening and asking questions would be a great help. This is actually very easy to do as the pressure and obligation to talk shift to the other person. Also, if you are the shy type, then you can also use this technique. When you talk about the other person's interest, you should also learn to be appreciative and give compliments. A common mistake is not to give a pleasant response to a person who shared something with you. In order not to make them feel ignored or unappreciated, you should express your appreciation by giving positive feedbacks or compliments. Of course, you are also free to give a negative feedback provided that you have a good intention of doing so. If ever you need to give a negative feedback, be careful with how you express it.

Be as polite as possible and avoid hurting the feelings of the other person.

This practice is also encouraged if the conversation starts to become boring. This is also a good technique to use during your first meeting or simply as a way to make the other person feel more relaxed and at ease with you. Just one thing that you should remember: When you use this technique, do it sincerely.

Relax, Laugh, and be Comfortable

Improving your social life should be a fun and exciting adventure. Therefore, do not be too hard on yourself and learn to just relax, laugh, and be comfortable. If you are stressed or pressured, then it will be hard for you to learn. But, if maintain positive qualities like kindness and peace and keep a positive outlook, then the easier it will be for you to learn and grow.

Committing mistakes is part of the development process. Feel free to laugh at your mistakes but be sure to learn from them. Remember that every encounter, meeting, or experience, is another opportunity for you to learn something valuable. But, it is important that you to learn in a positive and enjoyable atmosphere; otherwise, you might get tired and lose your enthusiasm. Since this is a life-long journey, it is only right that you also enjoy the journey. You cannot afford to be too tensed or pressured. Instead, you have to relax and enjoy what you do.

It is difficult, if not impossible, to make the other person feel comfortable with you if you do not feel comfortable yourself, just as it is hard to make a person laugh if you do not laugh. As you can see, the way you express yourself reflects itself on other people. If you want people to be relaxed when they talk to you, and if you want them to laugh and be comfortable with you, then you need to show and express these qualities. Remember the law of attraction and how like attracts like.

From time to time, you may meet people who would make you feel uncomfortable. If ever you find yourself in this situation, simply assess yourself and understand what it is about the person that makes you feel uncomfortable. This is a good chance for you to discover more about yourself. Do not be like the others who ignore opportunities for self-improvement. In fact, every encounter is an opportunity to learn more about yourself and be a better person. When you feel pressured, remember to relax and just be yourself. You do not need to please the people around you. Rather, just be yourself, and be the best person you can be.

Use Positive Actions to Express Yourself

In expressing yourself, you should be aware that intentions alone are not enough. For you to deliver a clear message, you should express yourself using positive actions. Whether through words and or gestures, you need to do something.

Without resorting to positive actions, then even your good intentions will remain hidden. The worst part about this is that there is no way for the other person to know that you even have a good intention. Hence, it is almost as if you did not have any intention at all. Keep in mind that expressing yourself always involves positive actions on your part. If you want to deliver a clear-cut message, then you need to do something about it so you can express it well.

Mastery of the techniques is also about applying the techniques in your daily life. In fact, it is full of positive actions. Without actions, change is also impossible to achieve. To connect with people, you need to do something, be it by word, deed, or both. You cannot express yourself clearly through inaction. Therefore, if you want to improve your social life, tell yourself that you should not be lazy and prepare to take actions.

This is also why improving your social life is an interesting adventure as it is a massive undertaking. It is when you have the initiative to take action will you be able to experience the good things in life. Unfortunately, there are people who get stuck at wondering what could have happened instead of actually making things happen. Of course, the only way to do this is by taking positive actions.

Reflect

Make it a priority to reflect on yourself from time to time. There are many lessons and realizations that you can learn by reflecting on your actions. However, it should be noted that the way you reflect on them also matters. When you reflect on your actions, remember to always keep an open mind. You should also learn to recognize your weaknesses. Unfortunately, there are people who don't want to acknowledge their weaknesses. As a result, they fail to correct these weaknesses and do not improve. Reflecting on your actions also presents an opportunity to discover new and better ways to socialize with people.

Every technique and encounter can be the subject of your reflection. It is also advised that you learn to view things from a fresh perspective that is free from any form of bias and prejudice. Learn to see things simply as they are. Sometimes it is all just a matter of changing your perspective or angle to get a better view of a situation.

When you make reflections, you should be as specific as possible. Also, be sure that when you are done reflecting on a certain plan or realization, you must take positive action. Again, without positive actions, it is difficult, if not impossible, to make positive changes. This is why it is encouraged that every realization or lesson should always be accompanied by the initiative to take positive actions.

Whenever possible, try to reflect on yourself regularly. A good time to reflect is in the evening just before bed. However, if this is not possible, then any other time will also be fine. Think about your day and all your social interactions on that day. Is there anything that you could have done to improve them? Did you do something that prevented people from connecting with you? Consider all these things and other similar thoughts and ideas, and try to learn as much as you can. When you reflect on yourself, it is important that you should be very honest with yourself, especially with respect to the mistakes that you might have committed. This is an important part of the learning process.

Always spend the time to reflect. Be honest with yourself and try to learn as much as you can. Indeed, regular practice of this technique will allow you to make numerous realizations that can significantly help you become a better person. The more that you reflect the better you will get at realizing the different aspects of your life. If you are not used to reflecting or deeply contemplating, then you might not experience its benefits right away.

Just like learning any other new skill or technique, just give yourself more time to adjust until you get the hang of it. After some time, you will soon appreciate just how important and helpful it is to do it. It is also a good idea to write down your thoughts in your personal journal or diary. This way you can keep a record of your realizations and developments.

Reflecting on yourself can also help you learn how to avoid mistakes. Indeed, many blunders in one's social life happen because of poor contemplation. Hence, it can help save you from losing a good relationship. It is also a great way to learn new things and gain valuable experience along the way. Just keep in mind that when you take positive actions, you also need to take a break from time to time and reflect on it.

Chapter 4: Common Pitfalls

Overthinking

Avoid the habit of thinking too much. This is another reason why you should pay attention to your train of thoughts. If you catch yourself overthinking or worrying, then you should tell yourself to stop. There is a big difference between actually applying the techniques and thinking of applying the techniques. When you apply the techniques, you do not think about them. Instead, you put the theory into practice.

If you haven't noticed it yet, all the techniques do not have complicated instructions. You should not forget that socializing is common and normal for a human being, and so you do not need to exert extraordinary efforts to accomplish this task. Hence, there is absolutely no good reason for you to think too much.

If you do not understand a particular technique, feel free to read the explanation over and over again until you understand it. Once you have a good understanding of the technique, then the only thing left to do would be to put it into practice.

It is noteworthy that even if you know the techniques, it usually takes time before you can apply them properly. Take note that this does not mean that you should not think; rather, just avoid overthinking as it is not helpful, and it only gives additional stress.

Overthinking is associated with worrying. If you think about something thrice, that is still normal. However, if you think and worry about it for the tenth time or more, then that is already overthinking and worrying, Also, most of the time, it is no longer helpful for you, and that is also where the activity of thinking becomes stressful and this is what you should avoid.

Always explaining yourself

Stop explaining to people. You have no obligation to justify whatever you do. Many people worry about what others might think or say of them that they end up explaining. Here is what you should remember: You do not have to explain anything to anyone. Just be yourself and continue to improve.

In fact, there are times when you do not even have to explain even to yourself. For example, once you understand a technique and know that it is good for you, then you do not have to come up with reasons to justify yourself. Instead, you can use that energy in learning the technique. Hence, realize that you do not have to explain yourself to anyone and that you have so many things to learn and do. Do not waste your time.

It is good to think and come up with explanations when you honestly feel that you want to understand something. But, once you already have the understanding, know that you do not have to make other people understand you. After all, your real friends do not need for you to explain anything as they would always think kindly of you, while those who are not really your friends can always think badly about you despite giving them every reason and explanation you can come up with. So, do not worry about other people; after all, they are always outside of your control. Focus on yourself and on improving yourself. As the saying goes, "When people say bad things about you, live in a way that no one will believe them."

Exerting Too Much Effort

This is a common mistake. Sometimes when you badly want to learn a technique, you would spend as much time on it as you can just to learn it. Although this is a good sign as it shows your dedication and commitment, as well as your determination to learn, this can also be a problem. Do not forget that time is an essential element. No matter how eager you are to learn a technique, you also need to give yourself enough time to adjust.

Also, by exerting too much effort, you only put unnecessary strain and pressure on yourself. This can make you grow anxious in the long run. You have to realize that you do not have to exert too much effort. Again, socializing is normal for humans. You simply have to learn certain effective techniques in order to improve your social life. Don't be too hard on yourself.

Of course, you need to be careful about being lazy. It is important that you strike a good balance between taking a break and exerting enough effort to learn the techniques. Hence, having self-discipline is important.

It is recommended you learn the techniques one by one. There are those who attempt to learn everything at once and then become disappointed at the lack of quality results. Again, do not rush the development process. If you find it hard to learn two or more techniques at once, then just learn them one by one. You can give yourself a week or even a month to learn a single technique. Once you achieve mastery, then feel free to learn another technique. The important thing is to keep on learning and improving yourself. Since this book deals with the master's techniques, then you are expected to at least be familiar with all the social techniques already as we have discussed in the previous books in the series. Feel free to go back to the other books and review the techniques, if needed.

Being Too Serious

Although it is good to be committed to what you do, sometimes being too serious can make you rigid and tense. When you socialize, take note that the other person can also feel or perceive how you feel, especially when you interact with sensitive people. Indeed, some people have a high level of empathy that they can easily 'feel' you.

Instead of being too serious, learn to relax and enjoy learning the techniques. After all, it would be hard to apply the techniques when you are too tense and under pressure. Take things light and easy. However, it is also not advised to just make fun of what you do. A certain level of seriousness is still required; otherwise, you might not learn and improve anything.

Focusing on the Result

Remember to focus on the action instead of the fruit of action. When you only concern yourself with the result, then you miss the present moment and fail to give it your best. Focus on what you are doing and be conscious of the present moment. When you listen to a person, be sure to give them your full attention.

Realize that as long as you stick to the proper application of the techniques, then the result will unfold on its own. However, in order to increase the possibility that your intended result would materialize, you have to apply the right actions. This is why it is important for you to focus on the actions as the final result would depend on them.

You should not allow your focus to be divided. The key here is to be conscious of the present moment. Do not think that the other person will like you and would want to have a good relationship with you. That is up to them to decide. Your only duty is to apply the techniques. You have no control of the fruit of the action just as you do not have any control of the future or how the other person thinks. Also, remind yourself that socializing is not about pleasing other people. Rather, it is about being yourself as you interact with others. Of course, it also means developing yourself and becoming the best person you can be.

But, how do you focus on the action? It should be made clear that there is a difference between focusing on the action and focusing on what the action would result in. When you focus on the action, you do not even think about *focusing*. Rather, you take the right and positive actions. This is the real meaning of focusing on your action and not on the result. It is about living, experiencing life, and connecting with people.

Manipulating People

Okay, although all the books in the series talk about techniques that can draw people and make people feel a certain way about you, it should be clear by now that they are not means to manipulate or control people. Rather, use them to improve yourself as a person and to effectively connect with people. Indeed, the intention matters, as well as how you make use of the techniques.

If you come to think about it, the techniques in all the books in the series are not a way to control people. In fact, they are all about you and improving yourself as a person. This is the basic key to having a good social life: Be a good person. Unfortunately, many people have forgotten and have been misdirected as to what it is to be good. They tend to ignore people when they talk and only focus on themselves. This book, together will all the other books in the series, reminds its readers of the good habits and practices that people appreciate. What is more, the books give you effective and powerful techniques that can help you become a better person to improve your social life.

Giving up

When it comes to developing your social life, one thing that you should not do is to give up. Do not be discouraged if you do not get your intended result. Again, many of these techniques take time and effort to master. If you give up, then you already prevented yourself from learning anything. Instead of giving up, you need to persist and continuously practice the techniques.

If you feel disappointed, don't look down yourself and take a break instead. By allowing yourself to take a break, you can come back to practicing the techniques with a fresh and renewed mind. This will allow you to learn the techniques more effectively. The key is to be persistent. Do not be discouraged by failures, even repeated failures, and mistakes. Instead, learn as much as you can from the experience and use that knowledge to improve yourself. There is no end to self-progress and development unless you impose a limit on yourself.

If you are serious about developing your social life, then you should be ready to face challenges. Mostly, these challenges will be about overcoming yourself. In order to improve one's self, then changes have to be made, and change is not always easy to attain. But, it is nonetheless doable and that there is no one else who can do it for you but yourself.

Whenever you feel like giving up, just relax and give yourself a break. The proper way to get a break is not to concern yourself with anything that has to do with improving your social life. Simply sit down, just relax and have fun. Do not even think about improving yourself or your social life. Normally, people give up if they fail to overcome a particular challenge. However, keep in mind that you only truly fail if you stop trying. So, as long as you keep on trying and giving it your best, there is no way that you can fail. Rather, there is simply so much that you can learn and gain. Therefore, never give up. Keep your enthusiasm and inspiration alive and strong.

Conclusion

Thanks for making it through to the end of this book. We hope it was informative and that it was able to provide you with all of the tools you need to achieve your goals whatever they may be. The next step is to apply everything that you have learned. So, it is time for you to achieve mastery of all the techniques and enjoy a more meaningful and happier social life.

As this is the master guide, you are also free to improve on all the techniques in this book and even develop your own. After all, there are no hard and fast rules to attaining mastery of over your social life just as there is no end to self-development. The important thing is that you have a good intention and that you always try your best in everything you do.

Finally, if you found this book useful in any way, a review on Amazon is always appreciated!